T0071742

HELEN MURRAY

NICK PAYNE

IF THERE IS I HAVEN'T FOUND IT YET

Nick Payne is also the author of *Wanderlust* (Royal Court Theatre, 2010), *One Day When We Were Young* (Paines Plough and Sheffield Theatres, 2012), *Constellations* (Royal Court Theatre, 2012), *Lay Down Your Cross* (Hampstead Theatre, 2012), and a new version of Sophocles' *Electra* (Gate Theatre, 2011). He is the winner of the 2009 George Devine Award for Most Promising Playwright and the 2012 Harold Pinter Playwright's Award. He is currently under commission with the Royal Court Theatre and the Manhattan Theatre Club/Alfred P. Sloan Foundation.

IF THERE IS
I HAVEN'T
FOUND IT
YET

IF THERE IS
I HAVEN'T
FOUND IT
YET

NICK PAYNE

FARRAR, STRAUS AND GIROUX

NEW YORK

Farrar, Strauss & Giroux
18 West 18th Street, New York 10011

Printed in the United States of America
Originally published, in slightly different form, in 2009 by
Faber and Faber Ltd., Great Britain
Published in the United States by Faber and Faber, Inc.
First American edition, 2013

Library of Congress Cataloging-in-Publication Data
Payne, Nick.
    If There Is I Haven't Found It Yet / Nick Payne. — First American edition.
      pages   cm
    ISBN 978-0-86547-770-4 (pbk. : alk. paper)
    1. Overweight teenagers—Drama.   2. Bullying in schools—Drama.
I. Title.

PR6116.A97 I38 2013
822'.92—dc23
                                                                    2012040669

Designed by Jonathan D. Lippincott

www.fsgbooks.com
www.twitter.com/fsgbooks • www.facebook.com/fsgbooks

P1

For Mum and Dad

I would suggest that even the most sophisticated and determined environmentalist . . . struggles with the fact that, under the shadow of future cataclysm, there is a life to be lived within the constraints of the here-and-now.

—Anthony Giddens, *The Politics of Climate Change*

Whatever we do today to reduce emissions will matter for our children's generation and beyond, but not for our own. The problem of climate is one of legacy.

—Gabrielle Walker and Sir David King, *The Hot Topic*

ACKNOWLEDGMENTS

In the United States: John Buzzetti, Jim Carnahan, Annie Funke, Michelle Gomez, Jake Gyllenhaal, Todd Haimes, Osheen Jones, Michael Longhurst, Brían F. O'Byrne, Jill Rafson, and all of the staff at Roundabout Theatre Company.

In the United Kingdom: Michael Begley, Pandora Colin, Pippa Ellis, Jane Fallowfield, Ben Hall, Ailish O'Connor, Josie Rourke, Roxana Silbert, Rafe Spall, Tessa Walker, Lily Williams, Kate Wasserberg (and all of the actors who took part in a workshop at the Finborough Theatre), and all of the staff at the Bush Theatre.

The panel of the George Devine Award for 2009: Lucy Caldwell, Chris Campbell, Harriet Devine, Bijan Sheibani, Graham Whybrow, Alexandra Wood, and Jenny Worton.

Minna, Mum.

Last, I would like to acknowledge the following books and their authors: *How Bad Are Bananas?* by Mike Berners-Lee, *What's Left?* by Nick Cohen, *The Politics of Climate Change* by Anthony Giddens, *Heat* by George Monbiot, *Six Degrees* by Mark Lynas, and *The Hot Topic* by Gabrielle Walker and Sir David King.

IF THERE IS
I HAVEN'T
FOUND IT
YET

If There Is I Haven't Found It Yet had its U.S. premiere in New York City on September 20, 2012, at the Laura Pels Theatre of the Harold and Miriam Steinberg Center for Theatre.

Cast

GEORGE Brían F. O'Byrne
FIONA Michelle Gomez
ANNA Annie Funke
TERRY Jake Gyllenhaal

Creative Team

DIRECTOR Michael Longhurst
SETS Beowulf Boritt
COSTUMES Susan Hilferty
LIGHTS Natasha Katz
ORIGINAL MUSIC AND SOUND Obadiah Eaves

If There Is I Haven't Found It Yet had its world premiere in London on October 17, 2009, at the Bush Theatre.

Cast
GEORGE Michael Begley
FIONA Pandora Colin
ANNA Ailish O'Connor
TERRY Rafe Spall

Creative Team
DIRECTOR Josie Rourke
DESIGNER Lucy Osborne
LIGHTING DESIGNER Oliver Fenwick
SOUND DESIGNER Emma Laxton
ASSISTANT DIRECTOR Ant Stones
COMPANY STAGE MANAGER Angela Riddell
DEPUTY STAGE MANAGER Dave Blakemore
SCENIC ARTIST Lara Etherton
DESIGN ASSISTANT James Turner
STAGE MANAGER (COVER) Xenia Lewis
PRODUCTION ELECTRICIAN Chole Kenward

CAST

GEORGE, male, 40s.
FIONA, female, 40s.
ANNA, female, 15. Anna is considerably overweight.
TERRY, male, 20s.

Ellipses following a character's name indicate a desire to speak but an inability to know quite what to say.

GEORGE: When I was younger, I adored polar bears. My, my father used to subscribe to *National Geographic*, and for years I had polar bear paraphernalia all over the walls of my bedroom—I even had a pair of polar bear swimming trunks. But not long after my wife had given birth to our daughter, I insisted the three of us take a trip to Edinburgh Zoo to see the last two polar bears in Britain—a couple, Barney and Mercedes, would you believe. But when we arrived—and I'll never forget this—when we arrived at the zoo, we were told that Barney had died: he had choked to death on a child's toy that had been thrown into his pool. So, so, I suppose you could say that my interest in the fate of our little blue planet began with a love of all things *Ursus maritimus.*

School corridor, day. ANNA *and* FIONA. ANNA *wears her PE outfit.*
    ANNA *dabs a tissue on her slightly bloody nose throughout.*
FIONA: Why don't we just start at the beginning? (*Meaning tissue*) Here.
FIONA *hands* ANNA *a fresh tissue and removes the old one.*
FIONA: Keep it pressed. Try not to dab it.
ANNA: I can taste it. The blood, in the back of my throat.
Beat.
FIONA: I used to loathe PE, you know.
ANNA: What?
FIONA: The horror, my goodness, the horror of having to get

7

changed in front of your peers. Everyone trying not to look at each other's bits—or rather, everyone trying to look as if they're not trying to look at each other's bits. Because who knows how our bits are supposed to look when we're that age?

ANNA: What on earth are you on about?

FIONA: I understand your frustration. But I just want you to know that in spite of all of that, it's important to try and remember—

ANNA: No, I'm being serious, I don't understand what you're talking about. None of this has anything to do with PE.

FIONA: Oh. Really? Well, that's strange, because I thought— Miss Clarke said to me that— If the fight wasn't about netball, Anna, then what was it about?

Beat.

FIONA: Anna?

Beat.

FIONA: Anna, please, I promise you I'm just trying to help.

Beat.

FIONA: Anna, they're thinking of suspending you.

ANNA: What? How long for?

FIONA: At the moment it's two weeks.

ANNA: What about Lucy Mitchell, everyone else?

FIONA: What about them?

ANNA: Are they gonna get suspended?

FIONA: Not as far as I know, no.

ANNA: This is such fucking bullshit.

FIONA: Language.

ANNA: Isn't it, though?

FIONA: Well. Perhaps if you tell me what happened, I might be able to help. But at the moment I'm completely in the dark— And you can tell me and I promise, you won't have to tell anyone else. You can tell me anything.

Beat.

ANNA: They found out you were my mum.

FIONA: What did they say? Anna?

ANNA: They just called you lots of stuff.

FIONA: Like what?

ANNA: Just. Lots of stuff, all right.

FIONA: And is that why you lost your temper? As opposed to it being about netball—

ANNA: Can't you talk to someone?

FIONA: How do you mean?

ANNA: Tell them it's not my fault. Tell them it's because you work here. Tell them what I'm normally like. That I'm not normally like this. I didn't ask to come here, you know.

FIONA: Anna (*doesn't finish*).

Beat. FIONA *watches* ANNA *briefly.*

FIONA: Why don't we finish this conversation off at home? There's soup in the fridge when you get in. And then I'll pick something up for dinner on the way home.

ANNA: What time do you think you'll be back?

FIONA: I might have to stop off at Granny's on the way home, but not late.

ANNA: What about Dad?

FIONA: Wait and see. (*Meaning nose*) How is it? Can I see?

FIONA *removes the tissue from* ANNA's *nose, wipes it clean with a fresh tissue.*

FIONA: Think it's stopped.

Beat.

ANNA: They called you a cunt. Lucy Mitchell and everyone. They said, "What's it like having a mum who's a full-time cunt?"

Family home, night. ANNA *is watching television, eating from a large bag of crisps.*

Doorbell, off. ANNA *turns off the television, hides the crisps and exits.* ANNA *opens front door, off.*

TERRY: (*Off*) All right? Hannah, right? Terry. How's it going? All right to come in?

ANNA *shuts front door, off. Enter* TERRY *with backpack.* TERRY *looks around the room. Enter* ANNA.

TERRY: Wallpaper's different.

TERRY *perhaps finds this a little amusing, but* ANNA *remains stone-faced.*

TERRY: 'S this a bad time?

ANNA *shakes her head.*

TERRY: Prob'ly shoulda rung or something, but. Phone was fucked and I thought, by the time I've arsed around getting change for the fucking. You know, the phone—and that, thought I might as well just. Anyway, sorry if all this is a bit out of the blue. Don't remember me, do you?

ANNA: (*Meaning yes*) No, no. My name's Anna. Called me Hannah—

TERRY: Right.

ANNA: But it's actually Anna.

TERRY: Right. Sorry. Only asking cos, y'know, me and y'dad, sorta sound a bit different and that, but—mean, some people find it a bit. "Brothers"? Yeah, brothers. Have to fucking explain it to 'em. Moved about a bit and that, y'have to fucking say. Anyway, I'm saying. Cos I mean, you're sort of looking at me as if we've never even fucking met. (*New thought*) Worked a treat, y'know. Whole niece thing. While I's away. This one bird, right, told her about you, told her about being a fucking uncle and that, and she went fucking; seriously, she went fucking. We get back to her place and she literally starts fucking (*demonstrates, stripping*). Mean, I was like.

ANNA: . . .

TERRY: So anyway, how's things?

ANNA *nods.*

TERRY: Yeah?

ANNA *nods.*

TERRY: Still at school and that, is it?

ANNA: Yeah.

TERRY: How's that going, then?

ANNA *shrugs.*

TERRY: 'S all right t'say y'fucking hate it, y'know. I did.

ANNA: It's not like the most thrilling part of my life right now, no.

TERRY: Fair enough. Anyone else about?

ANNA: Dad's out, but Mum should be back in a bit.

TERRY (*meaning what was she doing before he arrived*): Watching telly or something, was it?

ANNA *nods.*

TERRY: Any good?

ANNA *shrugs.*

TERRY: Put it back on if y'want.

ANNA: It's all right.

TERRY: No, serious, 's all right. Do with a shit, anyway.

ANNA *smiles a little. Front door sounds, off.*

FIONA (*off*): Hello. It's me, anyone in?

ANNA: Yeah.

FIONA (*off*): Do you mind giving me a hand with the shopping please, darling?

Exit ANNA. TERRY *is unsure quite what to do with himself while he awaits* FIONA's *entrance. He perhaps takes out some Rizlas, rolling tobacco, etc.—but then thinks twice.* TERRY *puts the tobacco, etc., away and checks that he's looking reasonably presentable. Enter* FIONA. FIONA *holds a number of sheets of sheet music and various other papers, also a shopping bag or two.*

FIONA: Hello, Terry.

FIONA *and* TERRY *kiss one another on the cheek during the following.*

TERRY: Oh, hiya, hi, how's it going?

FIONA: Very well, thank you. Yourself?

TERRY: Yeah, yeah, y'know. D'ya need a hand?

FIONA: Thank you.

TERRY *takes shopping bags from* FIONA *and exits.* FIONA, *alone for a moment. Re-enter* TERRY. FIONA *and* TERRY *perhaps smile at one another politely for a moment, neither quite sure where to begin.*

FIONA (*simultaneously*): Excuse the mess. If I'd have known you were—

TERRY (*simultaneously*): Sorry to just turn up unannounced, but—

FIONA: Sorry.

TERRY: No, no.

FIONA: Just apologizing for the mess.

TERRY: Don't worry about it.

FIONA: Been roped into helping out with the school musical. One of the other teachers had to drop out.

TERRY: Oh, right. How's that going?

FIONA: Busy.

TERRY: What y'doing? For the musical, which show is it—?

FIONA: *War of the Worlds.*

TERRY: Oh, right. Sounds good. No George, then?

FIONA: Is that a question or an observation?

TERRY: ?

FIONA: He'll be back at some point, I'm sure.

Beat.

TERRY: Listen, I'm sorry about. Turning up, but. Didn't really have anywhere else to—

FIONA: Mustn't apologize.

TERRY: Yeah, no, thanks, but—

FIONA: Honestly.

TERRY: Cheers.

Beat.

TERRY: So how's Rachel getting on these days?

FIONA'S *cell phone begins to ring (the ringtone is a pop song).*

FIONA: Shit, sorry.

FIONA *answers the phone.* TERRY *perhaps does now roll a cigarette during the following.* FIONA *perhaps throws* TERRY *a knowing look or two during the following.*

FIONA (*into phone*): Mum. No, it's not on tonight. It's not tonight, no. No, it's on tomorrow night. Tomorrow night; that's right. I've set the recorder to record it tomorrow night. No, you don't have to do anything. That's right. All you have to do is sit back and watch it. That's right. Yes, it's all very modern. (*Cutting her mother off*) Listen, Mum, I might have to . . . Yeah, that's right, I've . . . Okay. Okay. Bye, Mum, bye.

FIONA *hangs up.*

FIONA: Sorry about that.

TERRY: How is she?

FIONA: Other than the fact she's losing her fucking mind, fine.

TERRY: How d'you mean?

Beat.

FIONA: Better just make sure Anna's getting on all right.

TERRY: Sure.

FIONA: Can I get you something to drink?

TERRY: Beer'd be nice. Cheers.

Exit FIONA. *Enter* ANNA *with beer.*

TERRY: You not having one?

ANNA: I'm fifteen.

TERRY: Yeah, I know, was a. Was a joke. Don't worry about it. Didn't fancy being in y'mum's musical, then? Tom Cruise innit? *War of the Worlds.* Aliens. Well. Here's to it.

TERRY *toasts, drinks.*

FIONA (*off*): Will you being staying for dinner, Terry?

TERRY: If that's all right, yeah?

FIONA: (*off*): We're having mushroom Stroganoff, I hope that's all right?

TERRY: Sounds lovely!

FIONA (*off*): Anna, would you mind giving me a quick hand, please?

TERRY: Been a pleasure.

ANNA *smiles a little. Exit* ANNA. TERRY *sips beer.*

Family home, night. TERRY *is watching television, eating from a large bag of crisps and smoking a joint. He's possibly a little stoned now.*

There are perhaps also one or two empty beer bottles. Front door sounds, off. TERRY *stands, perhaps tries to make himself presentable (perhaps hides crisps, etc.). Enter* GEORGE *with briefcase, etc. (perhaps still wearing some cycling gear, high-visibility vest, and so on).*

GEORGE: . . .

TERRY: All right?

GEORGE *moves to* TERRY *and embraces him.*

TERRY: How's it going?

GEORGE: Did I, did I, did I know you were coming?

TERRY: No.

GEORGE: And are you, are you. Back, is this, is this, is this—

TERRY: Bit more complicated than that, but—

GEORGE: Of course, of course.

TERRY: But yeah, for a bit, yeah.

GEORGE: Not really sure where to begin.

TERRY: No.

GEORGE: Where have you been, Terry?

TERRY: Did ya not get the postcards?

GEORGE: I did, did you not get my emails?

TERRY: Not really that up on all that sort of stuff, to be honest with you, George. What about you, been all right?

GEORGE: There was one from Thailand, that was it, wasn't it?

TERRY: Yeah, yeah, that's it.

GEORGE: But you've been moving about, presumably, have you?

TERRY: Yeah, y'know, here and there.

GEORGE: Well it's good to, good to—

TERRY: Yeah. Yeah.

Beat.

TERRY: Bit late?

GEORGE: Yes, yes.

TERRY: Work and that, is it?

GEORGE: Yes.

TERRY: Y'still lecturing and that, then, is it?

14

GEORGE: Yes, that's right.

TERRY: House looks nice.

GEORGE: Do you think?

TERRY: Yeah, yeah. Greenhouse. And the attic, blimey.

GEORGE: We had it reinsulated. Lose a great deal less heat.

Beat.

GEORGE: Is that a cigarette?

TERRY: Fiona reckoned it'd be all right as long as one of the windows was open.

GEORGE: Wow, did she, did she really say that?

TERRY: George, 'course she didn't fucking say that, Jesus. (*Straight*) But I did open a window, so.

TERRY *offers* GEORGE *the joint.* GEORGE *is tempted, but perhaps first glances toward the entrance of the house.* GEORGE *takes the cigarette from* TERRY *and smokes.* GEORGE *coughs immediately—or if he doesn't cough, he is certainly surprised.*

GEORGE: Terry, this is, this is, this is marijuana.

TERRY: Is it?

GEORGE's *disappointment quickly disappears and he smokes a little more.* GEORGE *returns the joint to* TERRY.

TERRY: So Fiona was telling us y'putting together some sort of a bible.

GEORGE: I'm sorry?

TERRY: Fiona reckoned y'putting together some sort of book.

GEORGE: Right, I see. I see.

TERRY: Lot of work, she reckoned.

GEORGE: Is Fiona still, are her and Anna still awake?

TERRY: Hit the sack a coupla hours ago, I'm afraid. Stew for ya in the fridge, though. Lovely, actually. Loada herbs. Look, she told me to tell ya, but— Mean, she said if I was still up when y'got in, she wanted me to tell you to wake her. Up.

GEORGE: Oh.

TERRY: But, t'be honest with ya, she was looking pretty knackered, so I figure maybe 's best if I just. Tell ya. Now. 'Stead of waking her up. Mean, as long as y'don't mind hearing it from me and not her?

GEORGE *shakes his head a little.*

TERRY: Don't look so worried, George, whole thing sounds a bit of a mountain out of a molehill, know what I mean? Hannah 'parently got into a bit of a—

GEORGE: Sorry, sorry. Hannah?

TERRY: Yeah.

GEORGE: Do you mean Anna?

TERRY: Fuck's sake. Anna, today, 'parently she got into a bit of a fight with this other girl.

GEORGE: A fight?

TERRY: Thass right, yeah.

GEORGE: Well, is she, is she all right? Is she, is she—

TERRY: Yeah, yeah, 'course. Other girl took most of the kicking, apparently.

GEORGE: What were they fighting about?

TERRY: Couldn't tell ya.

GEORGE: I don't understand.

TERRY: Didn't really wanna dig that deep, to be honest with ya, George. "Hiya, good to see ya, been a year and a half, but hear y'beat the shit outta some bird today, love to hear more about it." Anyway, look, the long and short of it is, Anna's been suspended for a couple of weeks.

GEORGE: Suspended?

TERRY: Yeah. But it's all right, cos I've had a bit of a word and, y'know, me and Hannah, we're gonna.

GEORGE: I don't understand.

TERRY: Y'know, spend a bit of time together and that.

GEORGE: And, and, and Fiona thought this was a good, she thought it was a good—

TERRY: Gonna go to a couple of galleries, museums, that sort of thing. 'S not like y'gonna come home, find us snorting coke off y'skirting board.

GEORGE: Terry, please don't say things like that.

TERRY: All right.

GEORGE: I know you're only, only joking, but—

TERRY: All right, all right, sorry. Sorry. Anyway. That was it. Just thought it'd be easier if y'heard it from me. Evidently misjudged that fucker though, eh?

Beat, during which TERRY *offers* GEORGE *the end of the joint.* GEORGE *reluctantly smokes it.*

TERRY: So this book—

GEORGE: Yes.

TERRY: This bible—

GEORGE (*an in-joke that* TERRY *doesn't get*): I think the preferred term is "manifesto."

TERRY: Is it?

GEORGE: Possibly, I—

TERRY: Well, go on, then. Give us ya. Y'pitch, George, y'pitch.

GEORGE: It's very late, Terry.

TERRY: I'm interested.

GEORGE: Ultimately, I suppose it's a response to the failure of the Kyoto Protocol. Are you sure you really want to—

TERRY: Yes.

GEORGE: It's going to be called *How Green Are Your Tomatoes?: The Carbon Footprint of Practically Everything.* If the UN can't convince its member countries to reduce their GHGs, then I think ultimately it's about making people aware about, well, about what it is that they can— What it is that they can do. What it is that is within their *reach* to do. So the book maps out the emissions generated by, well, by—

TERRY: Practically everything.

GEORGE: That's right. A red rose, a pint of milk, a banana, a nappy, a leg of lamb, an international flight, having a child, a pair of shoes, a *vibrator.*

TERRY: Wow.

GEORGE: And I'm not saying don't do this or don't do that. But I suppose I am saying, Are you aware of the cost? A latte a day, for instance, equates to roughly the same CO_2 as a sixty-mile drive in an average car. For the same impact as one kilogram of organic out-of-season cherry tomatoes, a sixteen-stone man could eat his own body weight in oranges. A single cheeseburger a day for a year will generate just under a ton of CO_2. Everything, you see, everything counts a little more than we think.

Beat.

TERRY: What about weed? What's the carbon footprint of a joint?

GEORGE *stubs out the joint.*

TERRY: I'm joking, George, that was a joke. It sounds great.

GEORGE (*meaning to go to bed*): I should, I should—

TERRY: Yeah.

GEORGE *moves to go, stops.*

GEORGE: It's, it's, it's. It's good to see you, Terry.

TERRY: Yeah, no. Definitely.

Exit GEORGE.

Natural History Museum, day. Perhaps a temporary exhibition: intimate and colorful animal photography adorns the walls. TERRY *and* ANNA, *both seated.* TERRY *is rolling a cigarette.* TERRY *watches* ANNA.

TERRY: You all right? Had a look round and that? Y'mum reckoned y'might be taking some notes. D'ya need a bit more time? There anything else y'wanna have a look at, Anna?

ANNA *shakes her head.*

TERRY: There's not? All done, are ya?

ANNA *nods.*

TERRY: Can speak to me, y'know.

TERRY *watches* ANNA.

TERRY: Only tryina help, y'know. (*Meaning himself*) Mean, obviously doesn't hurt to try and get back into y'mum and dad's good books. But I'm saying. Didn't have to do this. Y'know, I could be. I could be. All sorts of shit I could be up to. And I'll be honest with ya, Hannah—

ANNA: Anna.

TERRY (*continuously*): Know 's been a while, but last time I was home, looked a little less (*puffs his cheeks out, attempting to demonstrate weight gain*). D'ya know what I mean?

ANNA: Can we go home now, please?

TERRY: I'm just saying—

ANNA: I'd like to go home now, please.

TERRY *watches* ANNA.

TERRY: Gonna have to grow up at some point, y'know. Mean, I don't wanna be all like, "By the time I was your age I'd already been up the chimneys for however many years," but I'm saying. People aren't gonna wanna hang out with ya if y'keep up this morose, sulky fucking teenage shit. I mean, maybe all this is part of the reason why y'haven't really got any friends, or whatever it is. All this, all this. Cocoon, shit.

ANNA: You don't know anything about me.

TERRY: Mean, what d'you do? Seriously. Like hobbies and shit, what d'you actually do all day? Mean, y'mum's doing that Tom Cruise show, sounds like the sorta thing y'coulda got involved in. (*Beat*) Fine. No, y'know what, fine. Sit here and sulk and go home and eat y'way through half the fucking house and see if, y'know, see if. Cos I'm trying. I am trying. Y'know what I mean, no wonder y'don't have any fucking friends. Look at the fucking state a ya.

ANNA *cries, silently.* TERRY *squirms for a moment, unsure of what to do.*

TERRY: You all right? Anna?

ANNA *sniffs, wipes her eyes.*

TERRY: Anna, come on.

ANNA: Couple of weeks ago, Lucy Mitchell and that lot poured a load of instant custard in my shoes and bag while I was getting changed for PE. When I told the teacher, she sort of just looked at me as if to say, "Well, maybe they just thought you quite fancied some custard?"

Beat.

TERRY: Maybe y'need to think about taking some lessons or something?

ANNA: What?

TERRY: Kung-fu or something.

ANNA: What are you on about?

TERRY: Saying. Next time one of these fuckers puts. Whatever. Saying, you could. You know, give 'em a good fucking kicking.

ANNA: I already did that. That's the whole point. I head-butted this one girl and they've suspended me for like two weeks.

TERRY: You head-butted her?

ANNA: Yeah.

TERRY: Properly just fucking nutted her?

ANNA: Yeah.

TERRY nods, considers.

TERRY: What's her name?

ANNA: Who?

TERRY: Girl, one you nutted?

ANNA: Why? Lucy Mitchell.

TERRY: Lucy Mitchell?

ANNA: Yeah, Lucy Mitchell.

TERRY: She a dick?

ANNA: Yeah, she's a right dick.

TERRY nods, considers.

TERRY: All right, look, do you a deal. You do whatever it is y'mum wants y'to do here and maybe one more place, and then, when we get back, we'll go into school and have a bit of a word with this. Girl.

ANNA: What?

TERRY: Saying. Nothing, you know, nothing. Just a quiet. You know. Friendly.

ANNA: I don't understand.

TERRY: I'm saying, if you promise to do some work here and at the next place, I'll go and have a word with this Lucy Mitchell and tell her that if she gives you any more grief, I'll be taking shits on her doorstep for the next month and a half.

ANNA *laughs despite herself.*

TERRY: Yeah?

ANNA: What about Mum?

TERRY: What about her?

ANNA: What if she finds out?

TERRY: She won't.

ANNA: How do you know?

TERRY: Saying. Who's gonna tell her? You?

ANNA *shakes her head.*

TERRY: Me? No. Lucy Mitchell? Is she fuck. There we are.

ANNA: I dunno.

TERRY: Come on. Few more notes here, few more notes at this next one. Then we'll sort this other thing out. Yeah?

ANNA *nods a little. She unzips her backpack and takes out a couple of pencils and an A4-sized sketchpad.* ANNA *stands, makes to go, stops.*

ANNA: Thanks.

TERRY *shakes his head a little. Exit* ANNA.

School corridor, day. FIONA *and* TERRY. TERRY *has a bloody nose, dabs at it with tissue.*

FIONA: Should keep it pressed. Don't dab.

FIONA *takes the tissue and demonstrates, holding it against* TERRY'S *nose.* TERRY *takes over and holds the tissue in place.* TERRY *glances at* FIONA.

TERRY: I'm sorry. Mean it.

FIONA: Yeah.

TERRY: This wasn't the idea. Just wanted to go and have a chat. She's pretty scared of 'em, y'know. Anyway, look—

FIONA: Did she say that to you?

TERRY: What?

FIONA: That she was scared?

TERRY: Yeah. I mean sort of, yeah.

FIONA: She said to you that she was scared?

TERRY: She said that they scare her, yeah. And that when it happens, when they're picking on her and shit, that she doesn't really know what to do about it.

FIONA *is a little taken aback by this, perhaps even a little upset, but does her best not to let on to* TERRY.

FIONA: You understand, though, don't you, that what you did, Terry, was—

TERRY: Yeah, no, I know. I know. And I mean it y'know I am. I am sorry. Only wanted to talk to the one girl.

FIONA: Whose idea was it?

TERRY: There wasn't like a plan or anything.

FIONA: I meant, whose idea was it that you come into school and—

TERRY: Oh, right, that was mine, totally mine. Anna, seriously, she had nothing to do with it.

FIONA: She didn't ask you to—

TERRY: No. No, not at all.

FIONA: You just said to her, then did you—

TERRY: Yeah.

FIONA: You just said—

TERRY: I said, What's the matter, why y'always moping about? and she said, she said, It's cos of these girls.

FIONA: And so you said—

TERRY: I said, Well look, fuck 'em, they're well out of order, why don't we just nip in there on the way home and have a nice little quiet, friendly, relaxed chat with 'em and see if we can't sort everything out? And anyway, so that was basically what was happening. Chatting to that one girl—

FIONA: Lucy Mitchell.

TERRY: *Outside* of school, I might add, chatting to her and then all of a sudden they're surrounding me like fucking hawks, fucking zombies.

FIONA: How many of them were there?

TERRY: Felt like a flock of the fuckers.

FIONA: All girls?

TERRY: At first, yeah. Fucking shouting their heads off. Some of the language—

FIONA: I know.

TERRY: Mean seriously, I'm not exactly Mother fuckin' Teresa, but I mean, Jesus, you wouldn't wanna invite a single one of those fuckers over for dinner, would ya?

FIONA *perhaps smiles ever so slightly.*

TERRY: Wouldya, though?

FIONA: Possibly not, no.

TERRY: And so, anyway, I'm just about able to handle these fucking. *Girls.* But then this one spotty little fucker—

FIONA: James Allen.

TERRY: Well he comes forward and he starts saying aren't I a bit old to be. Y'know, hanging around the fucking playground and that. And so I said he better watch who he's fucking talking to cos this isn't exactly any of his fucking business.

FIONA: I'm assuming he didn't take too well to being told—

TERRY: Fuck knows. Fuck knows what his fucking problem was.

FIONA: And had there been any physical contact between the two of you prior to the head-butt, or did the—?

TERRY: Sort of a bit of shoving.

FIONA: A bit of shoving?

TERRY: Yeah. Sort of.

FIONA: He shoved you or you shoved—

TERRY: Basically, I was just about finished talking to this one girl—to be fair to her, she sorta seemed to be okay about it all—but in the back of my ear, back of my fucking ear, all I can hear is this whiny little.

FIONA: James Allen.

TERRY: And so I just (*demonstrates "head-butted him"*). But I'd been trying so hard, serious, so hard to just. Keep a cool head. And I do, I hate it. Hate feeling that way. Fucking anger. Is he all right, then, or what?

FIONA: His nose looks like a plum, apparently.

TERRY: Anna's not gonna get in shit about this?

FIONA: I wouldn't have thought so, no.

TERRY: Are you? Just gotta tell 'em that it was all me. I talked her into it, I brought her down here. And I mean, it wasn't even like technically on school property.

FIONA: Yeah.

TERRY *watches* FIONA *briefly.* TERRY *takes the tissue away from his nose.* FIONA *takes another tissue from her pocket and cleans up* TERRY'*s nose, etc.*

TERRY: So d'ya reckon they're gonna wanna press charges, or what?

FIONA: Who knows. I don't think it's something we should worry about. At least not yet.

TERRY: Fuck's sake.

Beat.

TERRY: Is Anna all right?

FIONA: She's fine. Think she quite enjoyed it all.

TERRY: So how long's all this been going on for, then?

FIONA: How long's what been going on for?

TERRY: The bullying and shit.

FIONA: Awhile. I think. It's hard to know, exactly. I thought bringing her here might. I thought that it might help. But.

TERRY *waits for* FIONA *to finish.*

TERRY: What?

FIONA *shakes her head a little.*

TERRY: No, go on, what?

FIONA: I keep thinking to myself (*doesn't finish*). I can't think of the last time Anna brought someone home, you know? For dinner. A friend. And sometimes I think, Is it me? Have I

single-handedly turned my only child into an antisocial, overweight loner?

TERRY: 'Course you haven't. Listen, 'course you fucking haven't.

FIONA: When we're at home together, I feel as if she resents me
because I'm her teacher, and when we're at school together, I
feel as if she resents me because I'm her mum.

TERRY: Kids're cunts.

FIONA: I think it's possibly a little more complicated than that,
but thank you.

TERRY: No, but I'm saying. She might hate ya now. Y'know, fair
enough, she might. But I'm telling ya, when she's, when she's
fucking twenty-five or whatever, she is gonna turn to you, she
is gonna turn to you and she is gonna say, Mum, fuck me if
switching me from that other place to your place wasn't the
best fucking thing y'ever did. I'm serious.

FIONA *perhaps nods a little. Beat.*

TERRY: Listen, I hope this doesn't sound. But. Been thinking about
getting in touch with Rachel. And I just, guess I just wanted
to. Find out where you are. On that.

FIONA: Why do you want to get in touch?

TERRY: Y'know, just. Say hello and that.

FIONA: Were you in touch much while you were away?

TERRY: Couple of postcards and that, yeah. Listen, I promise I'm
not. Promise I'm not gonna—

FIONA: I know you're not, Terry.

TERRY: No, but I mean it. Over all that. But. I do miss her. Do. Just
wanna know she's doing all right.

FIONA: I think it's probably worth bearing in mind that. I think
she's probably quite happy where she is. At the moment. With
Richard.

TERRY *takes this in.*

FIONA: I'm sorry.

TERRY *sniffs, shakes his head.*

TERRY: I really love her, Fiona.

FIONA: I know you do.

TERRY: Fucking really, though.

FIONA: I know.

Family home, ANNA's bedroom, night. ANNA in bed, asleep. Enter TERRY. TERRY slumps to the floor, drunk. ANNA wakes up. TERRY is trying to roll a joint.

ANNA: Dad?

TERRY: Not unless there's been a series of very serious—

ANNA: What're you doing?

TERRY: Got a lighter?

ANNA: I don't smoke.

TERRY: Good. Cos's really bad for ya. That and drugs. Both. Fuckin'.

ANNA: Do you want some water?

TERRY watches ANNA.

TERRY: I knew you when you were this big, y'know. This fucking big. Serious. Now look at ya. No. No. You know what? Wanna know what? Gonna tell y'something. No, no, I am. I am going to tell you something and you, young lady, are going to listen.

TERRY gestures for ANNA to come and sit by him. ANNA does so.

TERRY: Now look, don't take this the wrong way. Cos at first might sound a bit. But. Saying. Fat birds, Anna, are the salt of the fucking earth. And you wanna know why, you wanna know why? Because you don't get fat by fucking. Taking it easy. You get fat by fucking. You know? Now I'm saying, you get a skinny bird in bed, you know what happens? They get all fucking. Slipping off their bra without you noticing, quietly sliding under the sheets and that. But a fat bird. A fat bird'll make a song and dance about it. And. It. Is. Beautiful.

ANNA: Terry—

TERRY: No. No. Because. Listen. Because. I'm saying. At the moment, y'getting a lot of grief. And it's hard, it is, 's fucking

26

hard. But what I'm saying, what I'm saying is, couple of years' time, couple of years', you watch the fucking tables turn. Because you are—

ANNA: Okay, I think you should stop talking.

TERRY: No. No. You. Are. Beautiful. You are. And fuck all those skinny cunts. Fuck 'em. Because they'll be married and doing their knitting or whatever and they'll realize they've fucked it all up. So fuck 'em. Fuck 'em!

ANNA *smiles a little.*

TERRY: I miss her, Anna. Christ, I miss her something chronic. Didn't realize how much until I saw her, d'ya know what I mean? And fuckin', fuckin'. Richard, fucking.

ANNA: You mean you went to see Rachel?

TERRY: Maybe.

ANNA: Did you go to their house?

TERRY: Fucking went there, yeah. Polite as fucking punch. Polite As Fucking Punch.

ANNA: What happened?

TERRY: Fucking, arsehole, fucking.

ANNA: Were you drunk? I mean, when you went there? I mean, were you drunk before you went there or after you went there?

TERRY: A little of both, thank you for asking.

ANNA: Did you really torch their car?

TERRY: The fuck?

ANNA: After Gran's funeral, did you really set fire to Richard's—

TERRY: Fucking hell. The rumor mill has been a-spinning. What d'you wanna do, Anna? With y'life. Because I'll tell ya something, little place like this (*shakes his head*). An' people love that sort of shit, outside the fucking baker's, natter, natter, natter. When Mum was ill, yeah, yeah, we were. We were, we were. And I, fucking, I fucking said, Rachel, I fucking, I fucking. And so, y'know, George has the whole, the whole fucking "just like his father," the whole fucking smooth fucking talking. All that shit. And George barely knew Mum, and that's, y'know that's. Whatever. But I did and I miss her and that whole fucking funeral was a fucking joke. Everyone wandering around, looking at me like I'm a. All of 'em, 'cept y'mum's cousin. All of 'em, 'cept fucking Rachel. And so yeah, she gets back with fucking arsehole Richard, you better believe I'm gonna torch that fucking car. Fuck!

TERRY *tries to stand. He gets to his feet but loses his balance.* ANNA *catches him.* TERRY *slowly puts his arms around* ANNA. ANNA *is hesitant, but slowly reciprocates. They hug.* TERRY *buries his head in* ANNA's *shoulders. They remain like this for a moment or two.* TERRY *breaks away, sniffs, and rubs his eyes.*

ANNA: Thanks for head-butting James Allen. I really appreciate it.

TERRY *bows.* ANNA *smiles a little.* TERRY *moves to* ANNA, *close, and tucks a little of her hair behind her ear.*

TERRY: Salt of the fucking earth.

Exit TERRY. ANNA *watches him go.*

Family home, kitchen, day. TERRY *is trying to cook a dessert.* ANNA *enters at some point during the following, unnoticed.*

TERRY (*mumbling, to self?*) "Whip together the ricotta, mascarpone, icing sugar, orange zest, vanilla seeds, and egg yolks until . . ." Vanilla seeds. The fuck are. (*Flicks through book.*) Fuck's sake. Fucking, Jamie, fucking—

ANNA: What are you making?

TERRY (*reads*): "Baked ricotta and mascarpone tart with chocolate and orange."

ANNA: Made that one before.

TERRY: Serious?

ANNA: It's nice.

TERRY: What's all this shit about seeds?

ANNA *moves to* TERRY, *looks through cookbook.*

ANNA: It's vanilla. You have to score all the way down the pod and then scrape out the seeds with the knife.

TERRY: Fuck me.

ANNA: Do you want me to show you?

TERRY: Go on, then.

ANNA *takes a knife and a vanilla pod and demonstrates to* TERRY *how to score it and remove the seeds.*

ANNA (*meaning vanilla seeds*): Try some.

TERRY *takes some of the seeds from the tip of* ANNA's *finger and eats.*
TERRY nods in approval.

ANNA: If I help you with this, will you help me find something to wear?

TERRY: Apron on the hook.

ANNA: No, I've. I've been asked out.

TERRY: As in.

ANNA: Yeah.

TERRY: Fucking hell. That's fucking. Isn't it?

ANNA *nods and shrugs.*

TERRY: Bloke from school, is it?

ANNA: Yeah.

TERRY: And he just called you up, did he?

ANNA: Facebook.

TERRY: Facebook?

ANNA: Instant message.

TERRY: What, and y'meeting him tonight, then, is it?

ANNA: Next week. But I just meant if I help you now, will you help me pick out something next week?

TERRY: Right. So is this ya. This y'first. Date. Then, is it?

ANNA *nods.*

TERRY: And he's your year is he?

ANNA *shakes her head.*

TERRY: He's not?

ANNA: Year twelve.

TERRY: And you're?

ANNA: Ten.

TERRY: So he's?

ANNA: Seventeen.

TERRY: Older, then?

ANNA *nods.*

TERRY: Blimey. Told y'mum?

ANNA *shakes her head.*

TERRY: George?

ANNA *shakes her head.*

TERRY: Look, I'm not. Don't wanna sound like. But. Mean, maybe y'should. Have a word with 'em, just in case. Look, I'm not saying y'shouldn't do it. Just saying. Be careful.

ANNA: He's nice—it's not gonna be like some weird Internet thing where I'm gonna turn up and he's gonna be this like forty-year-old bloke in a trench coat.

TERRY: Y'gotta understand, though. He's older. Gonna have certain expectations. Promise me something, Anna.

ANNA: What?

TERRY: If he invites you back to his place—

ANNA: It's just a date.

TERRY: Serious, though. He invites you back to his place, will y'promise us you'll say no? Anna. Please.

ANNA: If you promise not to tell Mum and Dad.

TERRY: Why don't y'wanna tell 'em?

ANNA: They'll get all worried.

TERRY: Maybe they're right? Serious.

ANNA: They'll freak out and they'll say no and I just sorta can't really be bothered to deal with all that.

TERRY: But what happens if it doesn't work out? Teenage boys are wild fucking animals, Anna, I'm telling ya.

ANNA: Meaning?

TERRY: Saying. He's a bit older. Gonna. Gonna *expect*—

ANNA: It's just a drink.

TERRY: Not when y'fucking struggling to walk the next fucking day, it isn't.

ANNA: That's gross.

TERRY: I'm just saying. Like him, then, is it?

ANNA *shrugs.*

TERRY: You had much. Mean. When it comes to. Y'know.

ANNA *shakes her head a little.*

TERRY: Definitely gotta watch y'back, then. Fucking literally. Anna.

ANNA: I'll be fine. And again, that's gross.

TERRY: D'you need any condoms? On the pill, then, is it? How old are you again?

ANNA: So have you spoken to Rachel since you turned up at her house and called her boyfriend an arsehole?

TERRY: How d'you know about that? Nah. Sorta why I'm. Peace offering and that.

ANNA: Have you made the pastry yet?

TERRY *shakes his head.*

ANNA: Should do that first. Do the rest while the pastry's in the oven. Have you got all the ingredients?

TERRY: Think so.

ANNA: Do you want me to help you make the pastry?

TERRY *nods.* TERRY *takes an apron from a hook on the wall, places it around* ANNA, *and ties it.* ANNA *begins cracking eggs (butter?) into a mixing bowl (perhaps the flour is already in said mixing bowl).* TERRY *reaches into his back pocket, takes out his wallet, and takes out a condom. However,* ANNA's *hands are deep in the egg and flour, and so she is unable to take the condom.* TERRY *slips the condom into the pocket on the front of the apron.*

TERRY: Just in case.

ANNA *continues mixing.*

ANNA: Did you and Rachel ever sleep together?

TERRY *nods.*

ANNA: Have you . . . ?

TERRY: What?

ANNA: No, nothing.

TERRY: No, go on, what?

ANNA: You're pretty experienced, I'm guessing?

TERRY: Dunno about "experienced." (*Attempting a lightheartedness*) Fingered a fair few. No, mean, y'know. I've.

ANNA: How old were you? When you first—

TERRY: Right, right. Fourteen? Thirteen?

ANNA: Young.

TERRY *nods a little.*

ANNA: Were you nervous?

TERRY: First couple a times. After that, sorta. All much of a muchness, t'be honest with ya.

ANNA: Even with Rachel?

TERRY: That was different.

ANNA: How come?

TERRY: Just sorta was. Got all the time in the world, y'do realize that, don't ya?

ANNA: Not according to Dad.

TERRY *nods a little.*

ANNA: Got a tin?

TERRY: ?

ANNA: Tart tin. Need to blind-bake it.

TERRY: Right.

ANNA: Do you know what that means?

TERRY: No.

ANNA: It means you bake the pastry in the oven for a bit first. Before adding the tart mix.

TERRY: . . .

ANNA: What?

TERRY: Will make sure y'look after y'self, won't ya?

ANNA *nods.*

TERRY: Good.

Family home, night. FIONA *is curled up in a ball, asleep on the sofa by TV light. Front door sounds, off. Enter* GEORGE. GEORGE *quietly kneels in front of* FIONA *and tucks a little of her hair behind her ear.* GEORGE *pecks* FIONA *on the cheek.* FIONA *rouses.*

FIONA: Hello.

GEORGE: It's, it's, it's. Late.

FIONA: Is it?

GEORGE: Nearly quarter to one.

FIONA: Where have you been?

GEORGE: Train was delayed. You needn't have waited up.

FIONA: I know.

Beat.

FIONA: We had our first *War of the Worlds.*

GEORGE: God, I, sorry, I completely—

FIONA: It's fine.

GEORGE: How did it, was it a, was it a. Success?

FIONA: Yeah. Yeah, it seemed to go down really well.

GEORGE: I'm really looking forward to seeing it.

FIONA: I'm looking forward to you seeing it too.

GEORGE: Well, Friday night, it's all sorted, Anna and I. Be there or
be (GEORGE *draws an imaginary square*).

FIONA: Don't forget about Mum.

GEORGE: I wouldn't dream of it.

FIONA: She called me twelve times today.

GEORGE: What was the problem?

FIONA: She wanted to know where I'd put the cat food.

GEORGE: I didn't know she had a cat?

FIONA: She doesn't. It died. She kept forgetting to feed it.

GEORGE: Ah.

FIONA: I'm not really sure what to do.

GEORGE: Well, if she doesn't have a cat, she certainly doesn't need
any food for it.

FIONA: I mean, I don't know what to do about whether or not to
put her in a you-know-what.

GEORGE: Ah. Yes. Well. You know what I think you should do? I
think you should come upstairs, and I think we should both
go to sleep.

GEORGE *kisses* FIONA: *a peck.*

GEORGE: Look, I hope this isn't going to sound . . .

FIONA: Go on.

GEORGE: Well, in the kitchen I noticed there was. In the bin. I noticed there was a tin.

FIONA: A tin?

GEORGE: Yes.

FIONA: I'm not sure I'm—

GEORGE: It was tinned pineapple. And tomatoes. There was an empty packet of tomatoes on the side.

FIONA: George, I've had an incredibly long day.

GEORGE: I know, I know, I know. It's these little slipups though, that—

FIONA: Slipups?

GEORGE: Slight as they may seem—

FIONA: I went to Tesco's, George. It's hardly whale-poaching.

GEORGE: Tinned pineapple, though?

FIONA: It was for Anna. I wanted her to have some *fruit*. Strike me down.

GEORGE: But, but, all the, all the lovely fruit and vegetables we have in the garden—

FIONA: I don't know if you've seen the garden recently, George, but—

GEORGE: Fiona, those tomatoes were from Spain.

FIONA: What?

GEORGE: We have tomatoes in the greenhouse.

FIONA: No we don't.

GEORGE: We don't?

FIONA: No. We don't. They look like testicles. The only tomatoes we have look like tiny green testicles.

GEORGE: I shouldn't have brought it up. You're still thinking about your mother—

FIONA: I'm not thinking about my mother—

GEORGE: Preoccupied, I mean.

FIONA: I'm not thinking or preoccupied about anything. I'm pissed off that you think I'm some kind of ecological heathen because I bought a tiny tin of pineapple for the first time in six months.

GEORGE: Why don't we go to bed?

FIONA: You know, yesterday I was cleaning out the spare room and I found a whole load of our old photos. Malawi, Trinidad, just after we'd gotten married.

GEORGE (*possibly not quite following where this is leading*): Okay.

FIONA: George, I wonder if we're not all due a holiday.

GEORGE: As in?

FIONA: As in a holiday, George.

GEORGE: Abroad, you mean?

FIONA: Abroad, yes.

GEORGE: All of us, you mean?

FIONA: Yes.

GEORGE: All of us, abroad. On holiday.

FIONA: Exactly.

Beat.

GEORGE: Fiona, I. The flight, I couldn't. I couldn't possibly. It would be hypocritical. Reckless, even. I'm sorry. Please. What about, though, what about the, the, the Isle of Wight? August, we could—

FIONA: George—

GEORGE: No, no, we could, we could, the ferry, we could. Be, be, be lovely. August, the Isle of Wight, be lovely.

Beat.

GEORGE: Fiona, when we were younger, we didn't have a clue what it was that we were doing.

FIONA: I know.

GEORGE: We were, we were, to say the least, we were reckless.

FIONA: I know. I know all of that. But still—

GEORGE: Fiona—

35

FIONA: George, I miss you. And I understand why you're doing what you're doing and I understand the time it takes. But there's a bit of me that's starting to worry.

GEORGE: About what? Fiona, about what?

Enter TERRY, *bleary-eyed, groggy.*

TERRY: Guys, sorry, I'm tryina sleep. D'ya mind (*gestures "keeping it down a bit"*).

Front door sounds, off.

FIONA: Was that the door?

TERRY: I didn't hear anything.

Exit FIONA. TERRY *perhaps begins to realize that he's about to be busted.*

GEORGE: Were we really talking loudly?

Offstage, some conversation and sobbing is heard, followed by the pounding of feet on the stairs and the slamming of a door.

GEORGE (*calling*): Is everything . . . ?

Enter FIONA.

FIONA (*to* GEORGE): Did you know about this?

GEORGE: . . .

FIONA (*to* TERRY): You told me she was asleep.

TERRY: . . .

FIONA: Terry, you told me—

TERRY: She was.

FIONA: I don't believe you.

GEORGE: I'm not quite sure I'm—

FIONA (*to* TERRY): She's upset. She's dressed up like God only knows what, it's one in the morning—

TERRY: All right. All right. She's been on a date.

GEORGE: Anna?

FIONA: A date?

TERRY: Yeah.

FIONA: With who?

TERRY: Some kid, I don't fucking know.

FIONA: You knew she was going, though?

TERRY: Look. She fucking—

FIONA: Terry, it's the middle of the night.

TERRY: I know, and I'm saying, all she'd said to me were that her and this bloke—

GEORGE: I'm sorry, I'm sorry, "bloke"?

TERRY (*continuously*):—were going to the pub—

FIONA: Pub?

TERRY: Yeah, the pub, that her and this bloke were going to the—

FIONA: Pub, that's right is it, they've been to the—

TERRY: Wetherspoon's. Just been to fucking Wetherspoon's.

FIONA: Oh, it's just to Wetherspoon's.

TERRY: That's what I'm saying.

FIONA: Oh well, if it's just to Wetherspoon's, then that's all right then, isn't it?

TERRY: Yeah all right, fucking hell.

GEORGE: Terry—

FIONA: She is a fifteen-year-old girl. I don't care where it is or who she is with, she should not be going anywhere near—

TERRY: Yeah, all right, all right, fuck's sake! I'm sorry, all right? She came to me and she fucking said, she said this bloke had asked her out, and I said, Are you sure about this? and she said, Yeah, he seems really nice, and I said, Shouldn't you tell y'mum and dad? and she said, no, cos you'll only worry, and so I said, Okay, but make sure y'look after y'self, and she said—

FIONA: How old is this bloke?

GEORGE: Well, presumably he's he's he's, he's someone from school, surely? Terry.

TERRY *nods*.

FIONA: I'm sorry?

TERRY: Look, why don't you just go and talk to her, 'stead of giving me the fucking—

FIONA: She has locked herself in the bathroom, she is so upset.

TERRY: Well, fuck me, if you were that worried about her, maybe you shoulda fucked off some of this other shit and—

GEORGE: Terry—

TERRY: No, no, I'm serious, giving me a fucking earache. You think I wanna have to be fucking wandering around, handing out fucking condoms fucking left, right, and center, like the fucking Pied Piper of sexual health? The reason she didn't want me to tell you, Fiona, is because she can see how much stress y'already under and she didn't wanna fucking, didn't wanna fucking aggravate y'any further.

FIONA: Terry, the reason she came to you is because I am her mother and she knows that this is something she shouldn't be doing—

TERRY: Ah, bullshit.

FIONA: And giving her *condoms*—

TERRY: Listen, I'll tell y'why she came to me, you wanna know why she came to me?

FIONA: No, actually I don't.

TERRY: She came to me because she knows I'm the only one who gives a fuck. You can lynch me all y'want, but you know and I know—fuck me, even George prob'ly knows—that that girl has been criminally fucking neglected.

FIONA: I can't listen to this.

TERRY: Hiding the Doritos in a different drawer and chucking the fucking Kit Kats on a different shelf does not count as fucking—

GEORGE: All right, all right, why don't we just—

TERRY: No. No.

FIONA: I think you should stop talking.

TERRY: Oh you do, do ya?

FIONA: I do as a matter of fact, yes.

TERRY: And why's that, then?

GEORGE: Terry, please, I, I, I—

TERRY (*meaning* FIONA, *to* FIONA): How d'you do it, George? How d'you fucking cope? Because it would do my fucking head in. Y'selfish.

FIONA: Terry, Rachel is petrified of you. And do you know why?

TERRY: Don't give a fuck, to be honest with you.

FIONA: I'll tell you—

GEORGE: Fiona—

FIONA: Because you are reckless and because you set fire to everything you touch. You are a scared, scared little boy.

TERRY: Still, least I'm not a dried-up old cunt.

GEORGE: Terry, please, God, there's just, there's just no need, no need, for, for, for. Please!

Exit FIONA.

GEORGE: Fiona, Fiona.

FIONA's *gone.*

GEORGE: I think you ought to go and apologize.

TERRY: Do me a favor, George, I'm not apologizing for shit.

GEORGE: You do realize I vouched for you?

TERRY: "Vouched" for me?

GEORGE: I told Fiona that you wouldn't be any trouble.

TERRY: I had no idea I was such a fucking burden.

GEORGE: Terry, come on, no one is saying that you're a—

TERRY: No, you know what? If y'don't want me to fucking stay, then I don't wanna fucking be here.

TERRY *makes to exit.*

GEORGE: Terry. Terry, for goodness' sake.

But he's gone; exit TERRY.

Family home, bedroom, night. TERRY *is stuffing clothes into his backpack.* ANNA, *unnoticed.*

ANNA: What're you doing?

TERRY: What's it look like?

ANNA: I'm sorry.

TERRY: Fuck're you sorry about?

ANNA: Don't leave because of me.

TERRY: I'm not.

ANNA: I mean, don't leave because of an argument that happened because of something I did.

TERRY: I'm not. I'm leaving because y'family are fucking mental.

ANNA: Where are you gonna go? Where you thinking of going?

TERRY: Dunno.

ANNA: Somewhere nearby, though, or—

TERRY: Dunno.

ANNA: When will I next see you, I mean are we—?

TERRY: Anna, I don't fucking— (*Stops himself*) I don't know. I'm not sure. I'm sorry. All I know is that I wanna leave.

TERRY *is ready to go.*

ANNA: I had a horrible time. Tonight. It was really horrible.

TERRY: I fucking said to you, Anna. Fucking said to you.

ANNA: Said to me what?

TERRY: Gotta watch y'self. Teenage boys, fucking arseholes.

ANNA: I went back to his house.

TERRY: . . .

ANNA: Think he was probably pretty drunk. I was all right. I'd only had, like, one beer. He started talking about. Asking me if I knew much about.

TERRY: Sex?

ANNA: I said I wanted to go home. I said it was really late and that I wanted to go home. But he said that I'll never know if I don't try. And it was sort of okay. Just about. But he started. Thought I was gonna choke.

Beat.

TERRY: See, this is the problem, with. Little fucking places. Like this. Got sex coming outta y'fucking ears, but everyone's so fucking repressed. Listen, I promise you, get through these next couple of years and soon as y'can (*gestures "leave"*). Get on the first fucking plane. And. World's y'fucking oyster.

ANNA: Don't go. I'll speak to Mum and Dad.

TERRY: I'm sorry.

ANNA: At least let me speak to them.

TERRY: Anna—

ANNA: At least let me try.

Beat.

TERRY: Listen, I'll be honest with ya. Reason I came back was because. And I realize now how fucking stupid it was, but.

ANNA: I don't understand?

TERRY: Rachel. Wanted to see Rachel. Wanted to sort things out. But y'mum's made it pretty clear tonight that ain't gonna happen. So. There's just nothing left for me.

ANNA *moves to* TERRY *and takes hold of one of his hands. She runs her fingers over the lines on the palm.* ANNA *holds on to* TERRY's *hand and looks up at him.* TERRY *tries to avoid making eye contact.* ANNA *kisses* TERRY's *hand.* ANNA *kisses* TERRY's *hand again.* TERRY *is growing uncomfortable.*

TERRY: Anna.

ANNA *kisses* TERRY's *wrist.*

TERRY: Anna.

ANNA *goes to kiss* TERRY's *wrist again.* TERRY *moves away. Beat.*

TERRY: I'll see you later.

TERRY *hesitates. Exit* TERRY.

GEORGE.

GEORGE: If I could scream from the hilltops that climate change is responsible for all of the hydrologic disasters we've seen during the twenty-first century, believe you me, I would. But attribution is almost impossible— So I can't— All I can rather politely say is that all right, okay, global warming might not be the *cause* of extreme weather, but it is certainly *intensifying* it. But given the position we're in, given the severity of the situation, isn't it time to acknowledge the fact that a planet which used to boast two polar ice caps is likely to end up limping toward the end of the century with only one? Or what it will mean for half of the world's population who live within two hundred kilometers of a coast if and when the entire Greenland ice sheet melts? Not to mention the decline of the beloved polar bear. The rising sea will not pick and choose its victims—And we can tiptoe around it or we can face it head-on.

Family home, night. FIONA *is perhaps pacing. Front door sounds, off. Enter* GEORGE. GEORGE *smiles at* FIONA.

GEORGE: Hello.

FIONA: Where have you been?

GEORGE: I was at a dinner.

FIONA: I called you. I left you a voice mail.

GEORGE: My battery died. I'm sorry. It died right at the start of the day. I don't have a charger on campus. What is it, what's the matter?

FIONA: Mum crashed her car.

GEORGE: What? How?

FIONA (*meaning* GEORGE's *dinner*): Why wasn't it on the calendar?

GEORGE: Fiona, what happened?

FIONA: She drove into a parked car. With a dog in it. She drove into a parked car with a poodle on the backseat. The owner called the police. He said she was trying to kill the poodle.

GEORGE: Do they know each other?

FIONA: They live next door to each other.

GEORGE: This happened right outside her house?

FIONA: When I got there, she was screaming at the police. I had to try and calm her down. She kept asking for Roger. She kept telling the police that Roger was on his way and that he was going to sort the whole thing out.

GEORGE: Roger?

FIONA: My father.

GEORGE: Fiona, I am, I am. So sorry. I'm going to buy a new phone. Two, in fact. Where is she now?

FIONA: I left her with one of the neighbors. I couldn't bear staying with her. I was shaking—when I got in, my hands. It's just so ridiculous, the whole fucking situation. Because in a way she's right: that little lump of a dog used to terrorize the shit out of that poor cat. And she was upset. She's an old woman, and she was confused and she was upset, and the police were just . . . rude, and I felt like screaming at them. And I know you hate it when I say things like this, but I just couldn't help thinking, Is that going to end up being me?

GEORGE: It won't.

FIONA: Because if it is, I want you to just have me put down.

GEORGE: Come on.

FIONA: Why don't you tell me about your dinner?

GEORGE: It wasn't very interesting.

FIONA: I'd like to know. It might help calm me down. Please.

GEORGE: Okay. Well—

GEORGE's *cell phone begins to ring—Nokia Spanish guitar.* GEORGE *instantly rushes to switch it off. Beat.*

FIONA: Um. I think you should probably leave. Um, because.

GEORGE: Okay, why don't I go on up first and then—

FIONA: No, I don't mean this room. I mean I think that you ought to go.

GEORGE: What? No— Now— Look— I'm—

FIONA: I don't mind you being late. I don't mind you working hard. I don't mind you having a ten-year-old mobile phone that barely works and that you don't even have a spare charger for. I really don't, George. But don't actively try and lie to me.

GEORGE: Fiona—

FIONA: I'm going to say good night.

GEORGE: I had no idea there was a voice mail, I swear to you.

FIONA: Good night, George.

GEORGE: Fiona. I.

Exit FIONA.

Council flat, kitchen of, day. ANNA, *in school uniform, and* TERRY. ANNA *has been egged; there are stains on her shirt, in her hair, etc.* TERRY *is scrubbing at* ANNA'S *shirt with a damp reusable kitchen cloth.*

TERRY: How many of them were there?

ANNA *shrugs.* TERRY *scrubs.*

TERRY: Mean. Fucking eggs. Is everyone at your school a fucking farmer, or what?

TERRY *scrubs.*

TERRY: You been home?

ANNA: What?

TERRY: How come you've not been home?

ANNA: I don't know.

TERRY (*meaning scrubbing egg stains*): Fucking pointless, shit's fucking dry.

TERRY *stops scrubbing.* TERRY *watches* ANNA.

TERRY: Anna—

ANNA: Have you got anything to drink?

TERRY: What d'you fancy?

ANNA: Got any Coke?

TERRY *nods, moves to fridge, takes out a can of Coke, opens it and hands it to* ANNA.

ANNA: How long have you been staying here?

TERRY: While. Been moving about, really.

ANNA: Whose flat is it?

TERRY: Old mate's.

ANNA: Thanks for letting me come over.

TERRY: Why don't I see if I can find you a clean shirt? Thing stinks.

ANNA: Can I wash my hair?

TERRY: Lemme see if I can find you another shirt.

Exit TERRY. ANNA *sips Coke. Enter* TERRY *with a large shirt.* TERRY *hands* ANNA *the shirt.*

ANNA: Thanks.

ANNA *begins unbuttoning her shirt.*

TERRY: D'you wanna go in the bedroom or something?

ANNA: I don't mind.

ANNA *resumes unbuttoning her shirt.* TERRY *turns around.*

TERRY: So is it the same group of girls or what?

ANNA: Sort of. Yeah, I mean sort of.

ANNA *removes her egg-stained shirt.* TERRY *turns around just as* ANNA
    is putting on the clean shirt and so turns back around. ANNA
    begins doing up the buttons on the clean shirt.

ANNA: Done.

TERRY *turns around.*

TERRY: Anna, look, are you all right?

ANNA: I'm fine.

TERRY: Serious, though. Cos I know I've not really been in touch,
    but—

ANNA: Did you get my voice mails?

TERRY *sniffs.*

TERRY: Yeah, some of 'em. Mean, phone's been playing up a bit, so.

ANNA: Did you get the one about Dad?

TERRY: How d'you mean?

ANNA: He's staying with Malcolm Wilson.

TERRY: What?

ANNA: Mum said it's for work, she said it's because of work, but.
    I don't think that's true.

TERRY: Wow. Shit. Listen, why don't I give y'dad a ring?

ANNA: What for?

TERRY: Just, y'know, think he'd prob'ly be keen to know what's
    happened to ya.

ANNA: Can't I just stay here for a bit?

TERRY: Anna.

ANNA: Just for tonight?

TERRY: 'S not my flat.

ANNA: Couldn't we ask?

TERRY: . . .

ANNA: I'm sorry.

TERRY *shakes his head.*

ANNA: That boy asked me out again.

TERRY: Serious?

ANNA *nods.*

TERRY: What'd y'say?

ANNA: Said no way.

TERRY *smiles a little.*

ANNA: You around next Thursday?

TERRY:. . .

ANNA: Wild Beasts have got a gig in London. If I could get tickets—

TERRY: Anna, look.

ANNA: I'll pay.

TERRY: Yeah, no, that's really kind, but—

ANNA: "Kind"?

TERRY: Anna, look, I'm sorry I've not, y'know, been in touch and that, but. I just. I think maybe y'mum was right. I. I shouldn't've let ya go out with that bloke.

ANNA: You didn't.

TERRY: Anna, listen, I can't look after ya. And I'm really sorry if I misled ya or—

ANNA: What?

TERRY: I'm moving back down to Weymouth. 'S where me and George were born. Years ago, but. Got a mate down there. Got this bar we been eyeing up. Y'know, thinking about—

ANNA: When are you going?

TERRY: Bit up in the air at the moment. But.

ANNA: Soon?

TERRY: Yeah.

ANNA: How soon is soon?

Beat.

TERRY: Anna, look, this isn't me saying. Y'know this isn't me saying, Thanks a lot, see y'later. But y'gotta understand, I. I. I fuck things up. And it drives me mad. Mean, Rachel.

ANNA *nods.*

TERRY: And fuck me if I don't look at you and I think (*stops himself*). Y'mum and dad really are the best people for the job.

ANNA: Yeah, I get it.

TERRY: Listen, why don't I call you a taxi?

ANNA *begins removing the clean shirt* TERRY *gave her earlier.*

TERRY: Anna.

ANNA *continues unbuttoning.*

TERRY: Anna, y'don't have t'leave straightaway.

ANNA *removes the shirt* TERRY *gave her and puts her school shirt back on. She hands* TERRY *his shirt back.*

ANNA: Thanks for the shirt.

TERRY: Come on, lemme call you a taxi.

ANNA: I'm gonna walk.

TERRY: Gonna stay in touch, y'know. Gonna make a fucking effort. Promise ya.

ANNA, *nods, perhaps beginning to cry—stops herself almost immediately, however.*

TERRY: Anna—

ANNA: Is Weymouth by the sea?

TERRY: Yeah.

ANNA: Do you miss it?

TERRY: Yeah. Sometimes.

ANNA: Is that why you're going back, 'cause of the sea?

Beat; TERRY *doesn't really have an answer.* ANNA *moves to* TERRY *and hugs him.* TERRY *is hesitant to reciprocate, but eventually does so, albeit to a lesser extent.*

ANNA: Bye, Terry.

They separate and ANNA *moves to go.*

TERRY: Anna—

She's gone; exit ANNA.

Greasy spoon, day. TERRY *and* GEORGE.

GEORGE: Really can't hang on any longer?

TERRY: Sorry.

GEORGE: I, I, I told her we'd pick her up from school and then all of us would drive to the station.

TERRY: I never said that. 'S not what I said.

GEORGE: I think she'd really appreciate a goodbye in person.

TERRY: George, we've already said goodbye. Already said it.

GEORGE *watches* TERRY.

GEORGE: Terry, where are you going, what are you doing?

TERRY: Fuck's sake, George. What happened to just wishing us good luck?

Beat.

GEORGE: A bar?

TERRY: Yes. A bar.

GEORGE: That's really, that's really the plan, then, is it?

TERRY: Yes, George, it really is "the plan."

GEORGE: And, and, and in terms of, in terms of paying for it—

TERRY: Something we're looking into, all right.

GEORGE: And if it doesn't, if it doesn't work out, what do you think you might—

TERRY: Look, fuck's sake, George! It's something I'm gonna try. All right? For the first time in God only knows how long, 's something I'm gonna try.

Beat.

GEORGE: And, and, and Anna, in terms of.

TERRY: Terms of what, George?

GEORGE: Still going to make the effort?

TERRY: Yes.

GEORGE: Stay in touch?

TERRY: You just worry about y'self. Fucking marriage, George. Mean, what y'doing about all that?

GEORGE: . . .

TERRY: Like to think I'm leaving her in safe hands, but I'll be honest with ya, I'm not so fucking sure.

GEORGE: Terry—

TERRY: Serious, George. Need to sort all this shit out.

GEORGE: I hardly think I need advice from—

TERRY: From what?

GEORGE: Why don't we just—

TERRY: No, from what, George?

GEORGE: I don't want to argue with you, Terry.

TERRY: If y'gonna call me a cunt, George, 'least call me a cunt.

GEORGE: No one's calling anyone one a—

TERRY: Aren't they?

GEORGE: Oh, Terry, please! Can't we just talk to one another for a change, can't we just talk to one another—

TERRY: What's y'daughter's favorite subject, George? What's her favorite meal? Favorite film, favorite band. Any of it. Stab in the dark, George. Need to think about what y'doing.

GEORGE: I need to think about what I'm doing?

TERRY: You do, yes.

GEORGE: It's I who needs to think about what it is that I'm doing, is it?

TERRY: It is, yes.

GEORGE: Terry, you you you blaze in here, unannounced, and, and, and within the space of I don't know how long, you you you rip a hole through—

TERRY: Come off it, George.

GEORGE: No, no, no—

TERRY: "Rip a hole"?

GEORGE: Yes, a hole—

TERRY: I barely scratched the fucking surface, let alone rip a fucking hole.

GEORGE: Terry, you called Fiona—

TERRY: I know what I said, George.

GEORGE: Well, well, well. I'm afraid I consider that a pretty big—

TERRY: I'm telling ya, George, if y'not careful, all this book shit—

GEORGE: I'm sorry, I'm sorry, "book shit"?

TERRY: That's right, all this book shit, I'm telling ya, if y'not fucking careful, it is gonna spell the end.

GEORGE: That is exactly why I am doing it!

TERRY: Ah, bullshit.

GEORGE: ~~Terry, I'm sorry, but~~—

TERRY: 'S just a book, George.

GEORGE: To begin with, but—

TERRY: Mean, who d'you think is even gonna fucking read it?

GEORGE: It isn't just about the—

TERRY: George, listen to y'self. What's the point in saving the fucking planet if y'own fucking family's struggling for—

GEORGE: Terry, we are hardly—

TERRY: Y'killing her, George!

GEORGE: Terry, the reason I am—

GEORGE *readies to leave suddenly.*

GEORGE: I can't (*doesn't finish "talk to you when you're like this"*).

TERRY: What? Go on, George, what? Say it!

GEORGE: The reason. The reason that I am. Doing any of this is not. Anthropogenic interferences with this planet's climate are, right now, right at this very moment, the single greatest threat to humanity. We have less than three decades to—

TERRY: What-fucking-ever, George. Jesus.

GEORGE: And you can, you can, you choose to laugh or you can choose to actually. Get off your backside and do something about it.

TERRY: You wanna know what this whole fucking thing reminds me of, George?

GEORGE: I dread to think.

TERRY: Mum. I'm tellin' ya, 's the same fucking thing all over again. It is literally the same fucking—

GEORGE: Why are you bringing our—

TERRY: Because she was thin as a fucking rake and she needed our help, and you buried your head in the fucking sand. And you're doing the same thing, you're doing the exact same fucking thing again. Go home and sort your shit out, George, because I am telling you, if you don't—

GEORGE's *cell phone begins to ring.* GEORGE *answers the call.*

GEORGE (*into phone*): Hello. Good day? Oh good, well, that's good. He's, yes, he's actually, actually standing right in front of me. No, I'm afraid we're not. I know, I know and I'm sorry. Yes, he's got to catch the earlier, the earlier. Well, I'm sure he wouldn't. Well no, hang on a, hang on a, and I'll—

GEORGE *holds out the cell phone for* TERRY *to take.* TERRY *doesn't take the phone.*

GEORGE (*into phone*): Sweetheart, I'm sorry, but he's actually just nipped to the— Anna?

GEORGE *ends the call.*

GEORGE: That was an incredibly unfair thing to do.

TERRY: Yeah. Well.

Exit TERRY.

Curry house, night. Slightly ropey panpipe music plays in the background. GEORGE *and* ANNA, *examining menus.*

GEORGE: I think it's probably for the best if we just don't mention any of this. I'm not asking you to start keeping secrets. But I did tell your mother that I would be cooking something. Maybe, perhaps, for instance, we could tell her that we stayed in and that we had, that we had, say, soup?

Beat.

GEORGE: I should have made something, shouldn't I?

ANNA: This is fine. It's nice (*meaning restaurant*).

GEORGE: It was recommended, you see. I'm told they source everything locally.

GEORGE *watches* ANNA.

GEORGE: One of your favorites, is it?

ANNA: ?

GEORGE: Curry: would you, would you say that it's one of your favorites?

ANNA: I don't have like a top five favorite meals, Dad.

GEORGE: But I suppose, just out of, out of curiosity, I suppose I'm just wondering—

ANNA: Dad. Relax.

GEORGE *nods a little.*

Beat.

GEORGE: National dish.

ANNA: ?

GEORGE: Masala. Chicken tikka masala, it's the, it's the. Officially the national dish of, of, of Great Britain. So my sources would have me believe, anyway. I'm sorry. Prattling on.

ANNA: It's okay.

GEORGE: I, I, I. I'm. Anxious, I suppose, about making sure we, you and I, about making sure we. Don't. That your mother and I, being apart, that it doesn't—

ANNA: It's fine.

GEORGE: I know you're, I know you're more than capable of, of, of. Dealing with it all, but—

ANNA (*looks for waiter*): When can we order?

Beat.

GEORGE: How're, how're things at the house?

ANNA: Fine, yeah.

GEORGE: Has there been any further word on your grandmother?

ANNA: Mum went to look at Vesta Lodge.

GEORGE: Vesta Lodge?

ANNA: Care home.

Beat.

GEORGE: I'm sorry things didn't work out too well with that date of yours. I'm not asking you to go into detail, but. I just wanted you to know that. Always, always more than happy to have anyone back. All you have to do is ask. Not, not at the moment, of course. In the future, for future reference, do, do feel free to. Always more than happy to. Boys. Not all the time, of course. But every now and again, can't hurt. Not overnight. I'm not suggesting. But for dinner, say. Or a drink. Soft drink. You know, when I was your age, I was actually, I was actually quietly petrified of women. And I think, really, I think really it was perhaps down to how little everyone talked about—at home, around the dinner table, for example—about how little everyone talked about it. Sex, for instance. That, that, that, most mystical of behaviors.

ANNA: Dad, please, this is weird.

GEORGE: Sorry. I'm sorry.

Beat. GEORGE *watches* ANNA. GEORGE *tries desperately to find something to say.* GEORGE's *cell phone begins to ring.*

ANNA: Do you think there's any chance Terry might—

GEORGE *receives a text message, volume on loud.*

GEORGE: Christ, sorry, do you mind, do you mind if I—

ANNA *shakes her head.*

GEORGE *takes out his cell phone from his inside pocket and checks the message.*

GEORGE: I'm sorry, I'm just going to have to make a quick. I'll be, I'll be—

ANNA: It's fine.

GEORGE *makes a call.*

GEORGE (*into phone*): Hello? Hello? Hello, Paul? I'm sorry the, the. Let me go outside. Hang on a minute and I'll go outside.

Exit GEORGE. ANNA, *alone.* ANNA *puts down her menu.* ANNA *looks around the restaurant.* ANNA *pushes away her plate.* ANNA *starts to cry, but stops herself.*

Family home, bathroom, day. Bath: taps are on, water is running. Enter ANNA. *She perches on the edge of the bath and checks the temperature of the water.* ANNA *turns off the taps.* ANNA *takes from her pocket a razor.* ANNA *dismantles the razor and takes from it two blades.* ANNA *begins undressing.* ANNA *now wears only her underpants and bra.* ANNA *looks down over her body.* ANNA *takes hold of her stomach.* ANNA *gets into the bath.* ANNA *pinches her nose and submerges herself under the water. After a little longer than is comfortable,* ANNA *reappears, gasping as she does so.* ANNA *takes one of the razor blades.* ANNA *drives the blade across her wrist.* ANNA *lets the razor blade fall into the water.* ANNA'*s eyes begin to water.*

ANNA *slumps down into the water.* ANNA *shuts her eyes.*

Hospital canteen, night. FIONA *and* GEORGE.

GEORGE: *Newsnight* have been in touch.

FIONA: Oh?

GEORGE: They want someone to talk about dog emissions.

FIONA: Dog emissions?

GEORGE: Domestic dogs. Dogs as pets. The carbon footprint of keeping a dog.

FIONA: I see.

GEORGE: Paul thinks I should do it.

FIONA *nods a little.*

GEORGE: Also had some interest from *The Guardian.*

FIONA: Really?

GEORGE: You remember—perhaps you don't—a while ago they published my piece about—

FIONA: Of course I remember.

GEORGE: Oh.

FIONA: George, of course I remember.

GEORGE: Oh. Well, no, I. Anyway, they're. Paul thinks we should pitch for an extract to be placed in *Weekend.*

Beat.

GEORGE: Also, I wanted to let you know, I. I'm hoping to try and reduce my hours at the university. You were right, I think. When you said. I've asked an awful lot of yourself and, and, and Anna, of course. And.

FIONA: Have you eaten?

GEORGE: . . .

FIONA: I only ask because if not, I'm perfectly happy to hold the fort—

GEORGE: Right, right—

FIONA: If you wanted to nip out and—

GEORGE: I see, I see.

FIONA: Think I spotted a Chinese down the road somewhere.

GEORGE: Chinese.

FIONA: Otherwise, back by the car park I'm reasonably certain there's a Tesco's.

FIONA *cries suddenly, silently, her head dropping to her chest.* GEORGE *takes a step forward,* FIONA *a step backward.* FIONA *pulls herself together.*

FIONA: Actually, if you do go to the Chinese—

GEORGE: Fiona—

FIONA: Sorry. I dread to think what the footprint of a sweet-and-sour chicken is.

GEORGE *watches* FIONA.

Fiona (*shuts her eyes*): I can picture her as a child so clearly.

FIONA *opens her eyes.*

FIONA: Keep thinking I should just. Leave. Work.

GEORGE: No.

FIONA: No?

GEORGE: No, of course, of course not, 'course you shouldn't have to. Leave.

FIONA: She means the world to me, George.

GEORGE: I know. I know. I know. I know. You know what we need? Don't you? You know what we, all of us, you know what we, what we need? And you were right, because of course you already, you already. We. Need. A holiday.

FIONA *smiles a little.*

GEORGE: No, no, we, we don't laugh, don't laugh, we. We do.

FIONA: Whereabouts were you thinking?

GEORGE (*plucking somewhere out of the air*): The, the, the, the Florida, the Florida Keys.

FIONA: America?

GEORGE: Yes.

FIONA: The Florida Keys?

GEORGE: The Florida Keys.

FIONA: And what would you like to do in the Florida Keys, George?

GEORGE: Well, well, now that you ask, I would like to, I would like to visit Mr. Hemingway's house, and I would like to, to, to. I would like to cook you both, yourself and and and Anna, I would like to cook you both a, a, a. Meal. From, from, from start to finish. Start to finish.

FIONA: What would you like to cook us?

GEORGE: Whatever you, whatever you. Want.

FIONA: What about the flight?

GEORGE: Well. Well. Well. I. Would. Swim. Instead. I would—

FIONA: Swim?

GEORGE: Swim, yes.

FIONA: Think it's probably quite a long way, George.

GEORGE: No matter.

FIONA: I don't think I could let you swim all that way on your own.

GEORGE: No?

FIONA (*shakes her head*): Not all on your own, no.

Beat.

GEORGE: Fiona—

FIONA: I might head back in.

GEORGE *nods.*

FIONA *watches* GEORGE, *lingers. Exit* FIONA. GEORGE *watches her go.*

Family home, ANNA's *bedroom, night.* ANNA *is reading* GEORGE's *book. Enter* FIONA *with Scrabble, perhaps hiding it behind her back.*

FIONA: What are you reading?

ANNA *shows* FIONA GEORGE's *book.*

ANNA: Have you read it?

FIONA: I have.

ANNA: Did you read the dedication?

FIONA: What would you say to a game of Scrabble?

ANNA: ?

FIONA *perhaps shakes the Scrabble box a little.*

FIONA *moves toward* ANNA.

ANNA: It's pretty bleak. The book.

FIONA: It is. Yes.

ANNA: Did Dad ever talk to you about it?

FIONA: Of course.

ANNA: He did?

FIONA: All the bloody time.

ANNA: Do you think it's going to do well?

FIONA: I really have no idea.

ANNA: I think it's probably going to be quite niche.

FIONA *smiles a little.*

FIONA: Probably best not to mention that to your father. Have you got anything planned for the weekend?

ANNA *shakes her head a little.*

FIONA: Maybe we could do something? If you like.

ANNA: Like what?

FIONA: Cinema, maybe? Not been to the cinema for years.

ANNA: How come?

FIONA: Not sure, really.

ANNA: What was the last thing you saw?

FIONA: *Titanic?*

ANNA *smiles a little.*

ANNA: Was that with Dad?

FIONA: It was.

ANNA: Was it like a date?

FIONA: A bit.

ANNA: Did he take you to dinner?

FIONA: He did.

ANNA: What did you have?

FIONA: Steak?

ANNA: Sounds nice.

FIONA: Have you spoken to Terry recently?

ANNA: Bit.

FIONA: Well, your father wanted me to let you know that Terry said that if you wanted to visit, he would really like to see you.

ANNA: Do you mind?

FIONA: Of course not.

ANNA: Would you come?

FIONA: Possibly not. But let's see.

ANNA: He said the bar thing's been going really well. Last time I spoke to him.

FIONA: Would you have liked a brother or a sister, do you think?

ANNA: You're weird.

FIONA: Why, why is that weird?

ANNA: Do you wish I had a brother or a sister?

FIONA: I don't know. Sometimes.

ANNA: Did you want more?

FIONA *hesitates, then nods.*

ANNA: You did?

FIONA: At points we did, yes.

ANNA: Why didn't you?

FIONA: Well. Because. Before you were born actually, we did. Try, I mean.

ANNA: What happened?

FIONA: Well. I. I miscarried.

ANNA: Oh. Maybe you should take Dad to the cinema again?

FIONA: Maybe.

ANNA: Or maybe you should just rent that film about the end of the world and stay in? Do you think you and Dad are gonna be able to sort things out?

FIONA: I would hope so. But. It's difficult.

ANNA: How d'you mean?

FIONA: Deciding what it is that has to change.

ANNA: Maybe it's me?

FIONA: What?

ANNA: That has to change.

FIONA: No. None of this has anything to do with you, you do realize that, don't you?

Beat.

FIONA: Have you had enough to eat? Still some more fruit salad.

ANNA: I'm all right.

FIONA: Why don't you come downstairs when you're finished reading and we can—(*gestures to the Scrabble box, perhaps shakes it a little*).

FIONA *moves to* ANNA *and embraces her, holds on to her. They separate; exit* FIONA.

Family home, day. GEORGE *and* FIONA. GEORGE *holds a small brown paper bag.*

FIONA: You'll make sure she wears her fleece. Won't you? If it's raining.

GEORGE: 'Course.

FIONA: She's really excited.

GEORGE: Well, good. Good.

FIONA: How's he been getting on?

GEORGE: Good, I think, good. Difficult to tell, really.

FIONA: How long do you think it will take to get down there?

GEORGE: Couple of hours?

GEORGE *watches* FIONA. GEORGE *reaches into a pocket and takes out an envelope.* GEORGE *hands the envelope to* FIONA. FIONA *opens the envelope.* GEORGE *watches* FIONA.

FIONA: George.

GEORGE: It's, it's, it's.

FIONA: George, you really shouldn't have—

GEORGE: I, I, I. Wanted. To. So. Please.

FIONA: Thank you. Why are there only two?

GEORGE: Well. Well. Good, good, good question. I'm afraid, in the end, I couldn't reconcile myself with the prospect of (*gestures "flying"*). So. So. Those are for yourself and Anna and, although a few hours behind, I will, I will be joining you via (*salutes, as if saluting the captain of a ship*).

FIONA: What?

GEORGE: Cargo. Cargo ship.

FIONA: You're going to sail to Florida? How long will that take?

GEORGE: Twelve days, but—

FIONA: George.

GEORGE: But, but, but there's, on board there's entertainment. All sorts of things. Buffet.

FIONA: Surely it's going to cost a fortune?

GEORGE: Well, it's a, it's a while away yet, so plenty of time to, to, to—

FIONA: Have you told Anna?

GEORGE: She, actually, she was the one who. Online. So.

FIONA: George, I don't really know what to say.

GEORGE: Well, you could, you could say (*doesn't finish "yes"*).

GEORGE *watches* FIONA.

GEORGE: I'm thinking about moving on from Malcolm's. He and his wife, they snore. It's horrific.

FIONA: I thought you were using the spare bedroom?

GEORGE: I am. I am. I've never heard anything like it. It's terrifying. I thought I was under attack at one point. Anyway, the. I was wondering if we might be able to start a conversation about. The possibility of.

Beat.

GEORGE: Is there something you're worried about? Specifically. Because we could address it.

FIONA: George, I think what you're doing is extraordinary, but you drive me (*playfully*) insane.

GEORGE: I know, I know— But I promise it won't be much longer, and then—

FIONA: There'll be a next time. And then a next time, and then a next time.

GEORGE: No.

FIONA: And there should be. Because you deserve it.

GEORGE: There's a balance, there is absolutely a balance. It all, it all simply needs a bit more work, a bit more. Organization. Doesn't it? Doesn't it?

FIONA: I don't know.

GEORGE *watches* FIONA.

GEORGE: Two planets. Next to one another. And, and, and one of the planets, he's ill. And the other, the other planet says to him, he says to him, "Are you all right?" And the ill planet says, he says, "No." And the other planet, he says, he says, "Well, have you been to the doctor, do you know what the problem is?" And the ill planet, he says, he says, "Yes, apparently I've got Homo sapiens." "Oh no," says the other planet. "I know, I know," says the ill planet. "Don't get me started." "Still," says the other planet. "Still. I hear they generally don't last that long."

GEORGE *watches* FIONA. *Enter* ANNA. GEORGE *and* FIONA *look at* ANNA.

ANNA: What?

GEORGE *and* FIONA *shake their heads.*

FIONA: Got everything?

ANNA: Yeah.

FIONA: See you later, then.

ANNA: Yeah.

FIONA *kisses* ANNA *on the cheek and hugs her.*

FIONA: Have a great time.

GEORGE: I, I, I brought you something else.

GEORGE *hands* FIONA *the brown paper bag.* FIONA *looks inside the brown paper bag.*

GEORGE: I'd like to sort the garden out. The greenhouse. I'm sorry it's in such a sorry state.

FIONA *moves to* GEORGE, *close.* FIONA *kisses* GEORGE *on the lips, softly, tenderly. They separate. Beat.*

FIONA: Safe trip.

Exit GEORGE *and* ANNA.

Weymouth Beach, Dorset, day. Gray clouds; the prospect of rain looms. GEORGE *and* ANNA, *overlooking the sea.*

ANNA: Are you any good at swimming?

GEORGE: You've seen me swim, haven't you?

ANNA: While ago, maybe.

GEORGE: I taught your uncle.

ANNA: How come you didn't teach me?

GEORGE: Not sure, tell you the truth. I think perhaps it was something your mother really wanted to do.

Beat.

GEORGE: You, you, you read the book, then?

ANNA: I did, yeah.

GEORGE: And?

ANNA: Yeah, I thought it was all right. Good. Thought it was really good.

GEORGE: And, and, and how did it make you feel? Reading about.

ANNA: I don't mean this necessarily in a bad way, but I guess yeah, it did just sort of make feel like we're all just sort of doomed. But then I guess that's sort of the point. I mean I guess it sort of made me feel pretty miserable, but I guess that's sort of the point. Is it all true? Everything in the book, I mean.

GEORGE: How do you mean?

ANNA: None of it's made up?

GEORGE: Not, not, not, no, not, not really, no.

Enter TERRY, *unnoticed.*

ANNA: Do you think he's going to come?

TERRY: All right. How's it going?

ANNA *hugs* TERRY. TERRY *reciprocates. They separate.*

TERRY: George.

GEORGE: Hello, Terry.

TERRY: All right?

GEORGE: Yes, thank you. Yourself?

TERRY: Yeah, not bad. Shame about the fucking weather. Listen, thanks for coming.

TERRY and GEORGE hug, a little formally, perhaps. They separate.

TERRY (*to ANNA*): Got you a present.

TERRY takes out a CD wrapped in an HMV bag. ANNA opens the bag to reveal a Wild Beasts CD.

TERRY: Not got that one already, have ya?

ANNA shakes her head a little. ANNA looks over the CD a little.

GEORGE: Why don't I get us ice creams?

Exit GEORGE.

TERRY: So how's it going?

ANNA nods a little.

TERRY: Thanks for coming down, and that. How long'd it take? No Fiona, then?

ANNA shakes her head.

TERRY: Oh well. Fuck her. Grumpy cunt. Sorry. Seriously, though, you, you feeling all right and that now, or what? Because. Mean, I'm not really much of a crier but I'm tellin' ya, when George fucking called me and he told me what had happened to ya. That was it. I was fucking. Gone. I'm saying: I'm sorry.

ANNA: Yeah. Thanks.

TERRY: How's things at school?

ANNA: Okay.

TERRY: Yeah?

ANNA: Yeah.

TERRY: Still getting grief?

ANNA: Not really.

TERRY: Not?

ANNA: I think once you're known as the girl that tried to kill herself, people tend to leave you alone.

TERRY: You got a fucking dark sense of humor, d'ya know that?

ANNA: How's the bar?

TERRY: . . .

ANNA: Is it open?

TERRY: Give us a chance.

ANNA: It's not open?

TERRY (*shakes his head*): Not yet, no.

ANNA: How come?

TERRY: This and that.

ANNA: What does that mean?

ANNA *watches* TERRY.

ANNA: Are you all right?

TERRY *sniffs, nods.*

ANNA: Are you really, though?

TERRY: Yeah, look, course. Just, bit hungover and that.

ANNA: It's not because of Rachel?

TERRY: . . .

ANNA: Her and Richard?

TERRY: How d'ya mean?

ANNA: Dad didn't tell you? Got engaged.

TERRY *tries to take this on board.* ANNA *watches* TERRY.

ANNA: If it's any consolation, I've not had much interest recently
    either.

TERRY: No?

ANNA *shakes her head.*

TERRY: Find that hard to believe.

ANNA *looks embarrassed.*

TERRY: Serious. Y'looking really fucking well, y'know that.

TERRY *grows upset.*

ANNA: Are you all right?

TERRY *nods.* TERRY *shakes his head.*

TERRY: What does she fucking see in him, eh?

ANNA: He's pretty rich, I guess.

TERRY: Fuck me.

TERRY *wipes his eyes.*

ANNA: Have you read Dad's book?

TERRY: Bits and pieces, yeah. You?

ANNA: Yeah.

TERRY: What'd you make of it?

ANNA: I thought it was really good.

TERRY: Yeah?

ANNA *nods.*

TERRY: Yeah. Shame no one gives a shit.

ANNA: What do you mean?

TERRY: Saying. Difference between actually caring about something and just being interested in it. Say we deserve what we get.

ANNA: God, you're full of shit sometimes.

Beat. TERRY *watches* ANNA. TERRY *moves closer to* ANNA. TERRY *puts his arm around* ANNA. ANNA, *after a moment, rests her head on* TERRY's *shoulder. Seagulls fly overhead and they both look up.*

TERRY: Reckon we might see a bit of sun if we're lucky.

GEORGE: I used to take a shortcut on my way home, when cycling from the train station to my house. A, a, a country lane, country road with, with a field on one side and a line of cherry trees on the other. One night—I think it, I think it must have been approaching midnight—I was on my way home and I, I noticed something. In the middle of the road. A shape, a body. It was a deer. Clearly very young, still very small. And it had, it had obviously been hit by a car. But it hadn't died. It was moaning ever so slightly and its head. Its head was. Twitching. Jerking, almost. And I didn't really know what to do. I can't leave it, I thought. I can't just. Leave it. Here. Like this. Before I could do anything, a car suddenly came roaring past. And another. Followed by another. And then more and then more. Slowly, the, the deer disappeared in front of me.

Now to get back, to get back to your question, up until this point I had been operating under the assumption that if people could only get to grips with what it is that needs to be done, they would of course be willing to change. Empathy, I thought, logic, would win out. But, but, but. Stood on the, on the side of that lane, I was hit suddenly by another possibility altogether. The most difficult part of this entire process has been having to grapple with the question of whether or not ours is a way of life that is worthy of preservation. Are we worth saving if we're not prepared to change? Anyway, I, I realize I've probably veered a little off topic, so. Perhaps now would be a, be a good point to hear something from the book?

GEORGE *puts on his reading glasses.*

GEORGE: If anyone has any more questions. Just.

GEORGE *takes a copy of his book, opens it, and reads.*

GEORGE: "Everything that follows is dedicated in its entirety to my wife and daughter."

GEORGE *turns the page and readies himself to speak.*

9 780865 477704